CURRENCY

TRADING

The Forex Professional's Toolbook

Alexander W.Russell

TABLE OF CONTENTS

INTRODUCTION

When I was younger, I was always fascinated by how things worked, especially complex systems that others often avoided. I became a very eager reader, always wanting to learn something new.

This curiosity eventually opened many doors into learning about economics. It started when I came across a book called "The Compound Effect" by Darren Hardy. From the day I opened the book, it had a profound effect on my life. It opened my eyes to see not just what can happen during a certain situation, but the extrinsic factors that can play into the end result of that situation.

Say, for example, you have two people. Person A and B. They are both friends from high school that played the same sport and had the same routine. Now they graduated and set off on their own paths.

Person A continues to exercise daily, drink plenty of water, and watch what they eat.

While, Person B gives up on exercise (or slowly falls off), parties on the weekends, drinks heavy amounts of alcohol, and does not get much sleep. These two individuals may not notice much of a difference in just a couple days, weeks, or even months. But over the course of a longer stretch of time, you will see a very noticeable difference.

It is not always the decisions that we make ourselves that have an effect on us, but the extrinsic factors as well. No matter how well we try to plan for something, life will throw something in our path, making it more difficult to get to your destination. When we experience these inevitable setbacks, it's up to us to assess the damage, get back up, and keep moving towards our goal.

In my economics classes, I was intrigued by the concept of behavioral economics, which is essentially the study of why people make certain decisions. This then led me to dive further into other psychology books. These books have helped my trading immensely, as I discovered that the market is extremely hard to predict. Let me put it another way, predicting the market simply can't be done with accuracy, consistently. This is where I came across a strategy, which I call my "Probability Based System," which we will discuss later in this book.

TRADER VS INVESTOR

Once you are ready to begin your career investing in the markets, you need to decide whether you are a trader or an investor:

Investor: Someone who uses their capital to put into a company that will reap future rewards, usually longer than a year.

Trader: Someone who is in the business of buying and selling frequently to make a profit.

I am mostly a trader, but there are times where I find something worth investing in, or something in which I see immense potential for future growth.

As a trader, I am looking for _High-Probability Setups_. But how do we find these?

In today's modern world, there is no shortage of information that is freely available on the web. Whether it is real or "fake news" can be difficult to tell, so I try my best to stay away from being exposed to too much information. Too much information can be toxic to your trading success. There are many traders, especially inexperienced traders, on Twitter or Stocktwits that spit out false claims or make obnoxious assumptions about where things are headed. They do this to hopefully change the minds of others to drive the stock price in their favor. Have you ever seen the movie "Wolf of Wall Street"?

Another dangerous thing to watch out for is people trying to sell you their trading algorithm. Why would you ever trust a robot to trade for you and that can potentially open a trade based on a false signal and drive your account to zero? They make it seem like it's as easy as copying someone's algo, plugging it in, and making tons of money. Trust me, if it was, I would have done it already and wouldn't waste my time writing this book. I would be sipping a rum and coke, laying on the beach without a care in the world, all from buying a $199 trading system.

After having read countless books on trading, economics, and psychology, I have realized that there is no single "holy grail" of trading systems, regardless of what you may hear.

This book was designed to cut through the noise.

I realized that when I was able to simplify my trading, and when I stopped trying to predict the market, my trading improved. When I stuck to the basics and developed a solid understanding of probability, the Law of Large Numbers, and chart patterns, that was when I became a profitable trader.

As I stated, this book is designed to cut through the noise, but I have included a good deal of basic to advanced material that I have learned since I started studying Forex. There is a good amount of information that you may not use, but I would highly recommend that you learn as much as you can if you want to be successful. It is certainly possible that you could come across an opportunity that everyone has been missing simply because you took the time and effort to educate yourself on a topic. Trading can be very complex and everything you end up learning will give you a new lense to look through. Every lense you develop will help you put the pieces together and give you an edge over other traders.

It is crucial for you to constantly educate yourself to be successful, both in this business and in life in general. It may not always be "what" you hear that is important, but also "HOW" you hear it, that can have a significant impact. I have learned things from people that I know I have heard before, but it was "how" they said it or presented the information that had a lasting effect on me.

Currency Demand

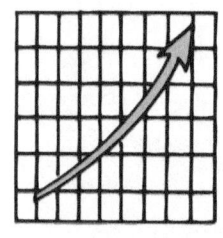

Price tends to rise when:

Demand Increases

Rate Increase

Circulation Decreases

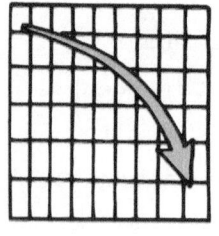

Price tends to drop when:

Demand Decreases

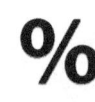

Rate Drop

Circulation Increases

WHAT IS FOREX?

Simply put, forex is buying or selling one currency for another currency. In forex trading, you want to buy the currency with the highest demand, while selling the currency with the lowest demand. The purpose for buying and selling can be different for different parties. Large corporations do it to conduct business with overseas trading partners, while individuals may get involved to buy products denominated in foreign currency. Traders and speculators do it to profit from short and long term movements in currency values.

HOW DOES FOREX TRADING WORK?

Forex is generally traded in three forms:

Spot Forex: This market refers to the purchase or sale of a currency at a current moment or in other words, on the spot.

Forward Forex: This market facilitates the trading of over the counter

(OTC) currency contracts. It is generally used by businesses to hedge their forex exposure.

Forex Futures: These are contracts in which buyers and sellers have agreed on a specified future transaction price and date. Companies such as airlines use futures contracts as a hedge against inflation in oil prices.

Forex Options: This consists of call and put options that give the buyer the right, but not an obligation, to buy or sell a forex pair at a predetermined price at a specified time in the future. An option seller, on the other hand, is obligated to fulfill the trade if the buyer chooses to exercise the right.

UNDERSTANDING A FOREX PAIR

Forex is quoted in pairs. For example, the Euro and the U.S. Dollar looks like this: **EUR/USD**

The first currency in the pair is called the base currency and the second currency is called the quote currency. While going long, you are buying the base currency selling the quote currency. When going short a pair, the base currency will be sold and the quote currency will be bought.
Let's say the EUR/USD pair is trading at 1.1100. This means that 1 Euro is equivalent to $1.11 USD.

UNDERSTANDING PIPS

A currency pair's movement is measured in what is known as "pips," which is generally the movement in the fourth decimal place of the currency pair

(with some exceptions like the JPY, which is only 2 decimals). So, if GBP/USD moves from 1.3139 to 1.3140, it means that the GBP has appreciated by 1 pip. A fifth place decimal number in a currency pair is known as a micro-pip, which is a fraction of a pip.

The exception to this rule is when a quote currency is listed in a smaller denomination. For example, GBP/JPY might be trading at 143.43, which makes a fourth decimal point move too small to trade. Here, traders consider the move in the second decimal place to determine the pip movement.

THE SPREAD IN FOREX MARKETS

Forex pairs trade in an auction market with a buy price and sell price. The spread, however, is the difference in price you pay between the buy and sell price. This serves as the broker's commission on the trade.

For example, if the buy price of **EUR/USD** is 1.3457 and the sell price is 1.3453, you are paying a 4 pip spread.

TRADE SIZE

Forex trades happen in lots, which means there is a minimum number of currency units that you must buy or sell. These lots are broken down into standard lots, mini lots and micro lots for traders to choose from:
Standard Lot: 100,000 units
Mini Lot: 10,000 units
Micro Lot: 1,000 units

WHAT DRIVES THE FOREX MARKETS?

There are many factors that impact forex markets, including economic indicators (GDP, Inflation, Employment, Wages etc.), trade, politics, monetary policies, interest rates, fiscal policies, geopolitics and news flow.

To be successful and trade profitably, traders should use a combination of technical, fundamental, and sentiment analysis to strategically position themselves around economic events.

Naive traders inevitably experience the temptation to trade on leverage to earn big profits from small movements. Because of this, many traders make big mistakes and simply quit Forex trading altogether. The keys to trading Forex profitably are to formulate a working strategy with lots of practice, trade with a manageable level of leverage, and actively manage risk by cutting the losses short. The goal here is to *lose less when you lose and earn more when you win*. You want to be on the winning side of a 50/50 chance.

A lot of money is made and lost in the $5 trillion daily Forex market. The 24x5 nature of the industry and the ease of trading with leverage makes currency the most lucrative market for traders. Like any other asset class, money is made in Forex by buying low and selling high (going long) or selling high and buying low (selling short).

As Forex is a worldwide market, there are few regulations that apply, and large international banks and brokers essentially act as market makers. These banks buy and sell currencies for their institutional clients, while the brokers make the market for individual clients. These individual clients trade over the counter and form the bulk of Forex activity.

*"If you don't find a way to make money while you sleep,
you will work until you die"*

- Warren Buffett

MAKING MONEY
IN FOREX

Here is the most important part of currency trading, how money is made. There are two ways you can make money in the spot Forex market:

1) **Pip Appreciation or Depreciation**
2) **The Carry Trade**

To better understand this, let's look at an example of the most traded currency pair, the EUR/USD.

1) Appreciation or Depreciation of Pips

Say you buy the EUR/USD pair at 1.1000 and the pair rises to 1.1100. You would gain a value of 100 pips for whatever lot size you traded. Inversely, if the pair decreased from 1.1000 to 1.0900, you would lose the value of 100 pips

2) The Carry Trade

The carry trade is the difference in the interest rate of the currency pair. For example, in the EUR/USD pair, if the Euro carries a 0% rate, while the U.S. Dollar is at 1.75%, there is a difference of 1.75%. This means you will have to pay the rate if you are buying the pair, or you would receive it if you are selling the pair.

FOREX TRADING STRATEGIES

Random buying and selling generally does not typically lead to profitability in the Forex market. To be profitable and successful, you need a strategy that consistently makes money for you. Your strategy could be based on purely qualitative factors like the economic well-being of a country, or you can work purely on quantitative factors like technical charts or a mix of both. Traders often deploy a host of strategies before zeroing in on one strategy that works best for them. As a beginner, your focus should be on formulating a strategy by testing different strategies based on your skill set, knowledge, and temperament.

CONCLUSION

Making money from the Forex market is more of a marathon than a sprint. It takes a lot of hard work and patience to understand the intricacies of the Forex world. You can learn how to navigate forex through practice over a long period of time, but it is also important to manage your risk and follow stop losses strictly to remain in the Forex trading game for a long-haul.

UNDERSTANDING
LEVERAGE

—— •▪ — ▮ — ▪• ——

"Give me a lever long enough and a fulcrum on which to place it,
and I shall move the world"
-Archimedes

Leverage is an important element in forex trading. It helps a trader magnify her exposure and take an outsized bet while only small amounts of capital by borrowing the balance from the broker. Forex traders get high leverage for trades due to the lower volatility and high liquidity of forex markets.

Brokers offer leverage in ratios of 50:1, 100:1, 200:1 and in some cases 400:1. In a 50:1 ratio, a trader can take positions worth 50x the capital needed.

The required capital for a position is called margin money. When margin falls short due to losses in the trading account, the trader receives a margin call.

EXAMPLE

Let's assume a trader opens a brokerage account which offers a leverage of 100:1. If the trader puts in $10,000, she can take a position worth $1,000,000. It also means that the trader needs to put in just 1% (1/100) to trade. Let's further assume that the trader takes a position in USD/GBP pair for the full tradable value of $1 million. A 1% move in favor of the trader earns $10,000, which doubles the trader's capital, while a 1% move against the trader results in a loss of the entire capital amount.

BENEFITS OF LEVERAGE

The obvious benefit of leverage is that you can magnify the size of your trade and, therefore, the size of your potential profits. Leverage is a useful weapon for smart and seasoned traders who can use it opportunistically to earn outsized profits.

DRAWBACKS OF LEVERAGE

The obvious drawback of leverage is that it can magnify your losses and wipe out your capital in an extremely short period. Inexperienced traders are at the biggest risk while using leverage because they seldom understand the downside risks and can be carried away by the upside potential.

HOW TO MANAGE THE RISK OF LEVERAGE

The best way to manage your risk in leverage is to not use it irresponsibly. You should not take a 100x leverage just because it is available. Smart

traders do not go beyond 30x in leverage, because the safety of their capital is of utmost importance to them.

You should also use stop losses and follow them diligently to avoid riding the losses that can put you out of the game. If you are unsure of your emotional reactions to incorrect bets, consider putting in stop loss orders to automatically drive you out of your positions when the losses are still manageable.

Keeping your trades small is also helpful when you are new to trading. It will be helpful because the cost of your mistakes will be small and manageable. Once you have learned enough and gained experience, you can consider increasing the size of your trades gradually.

REMEMBER

Leverage is an important element of forex trading. When used well, it can be a boon, but when mishandled, it can end your trading career in minutes. The quantum of leverage you can use mainly depends on your trading strategy. If you are a day trader and do not carry overnight positions at all, you can play around with high leverage, but if you are a positional trader, keep your leverage at manageable levels to avoid getting hurt by overnight movements.

Beginners should be extra cautious with leverage. I recommend starting small and learning while you trade. Then, gradually move up the leverage ladder once you know which trading strategy works best for you.

USD 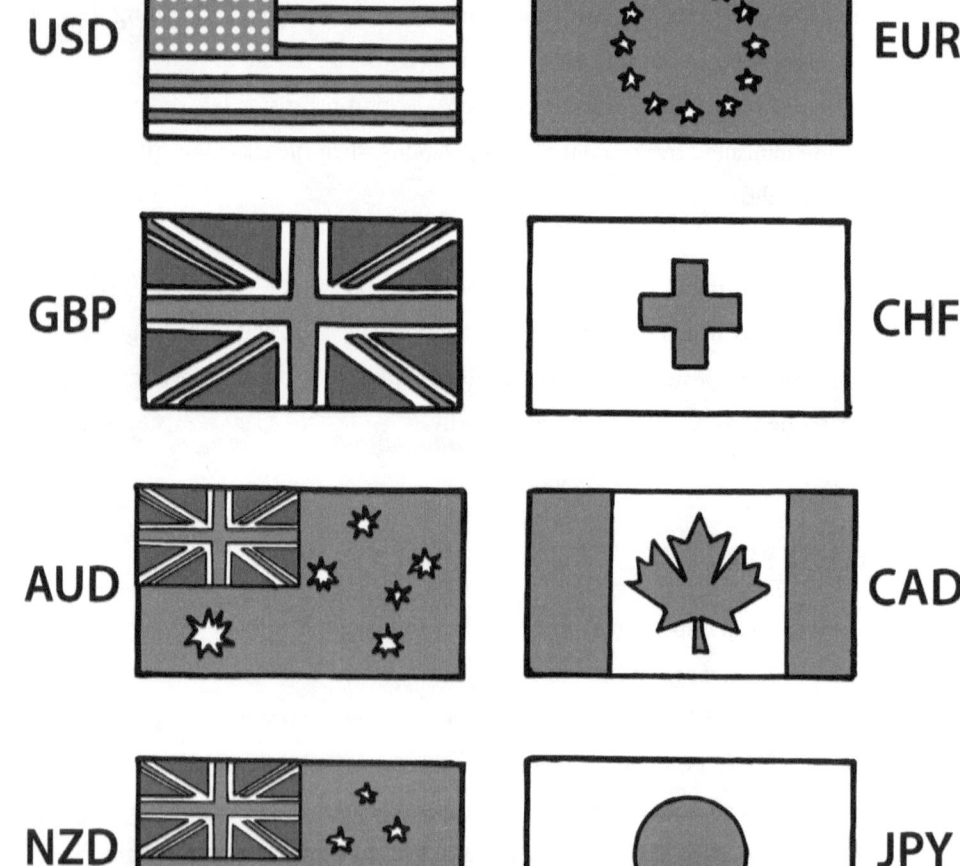 EUR

GBP CHF

AUD CAD

NZD JPY

BEST PAIRS
TO TRADE

The highly liquid FX market involves a turnover of roughly $ 5.3 trillion per day. It is open for trading around the clock on weekdays and has more than 150 currencies from countries around the world available for trade. With 64 pairs to trade, there are numerous combinations of currencies you can choose from. However, not all of these combinations are readily tradable. The market is skewed towards the top 10 currency pairs, which comprise approximately 85% of the total trading volumes in FX markets. We will take a look at the top 6 currency pairs you can trade with, but first let's understand some of the basic terms used in Forex markets.

Bid Price: The price at which you can sell to the broker.

Ask Price: The price at which you can buy from the broker.

Spread: The difference between the bid and ask price.

Currency Quotation: How much of the quote currency is needed to buy one unit of base currency. For example, EUR/USD represents how much USD is needed to buy one unit of EUR.

Base Currency: The first currency appearing in a currency pair quotation.

Quote currency: The second currency appearing in a currency pair quotation.

Pip: The smallest movement a currency can make.

Margin Money: Your initial deposit to the broker for FX trading.

Leverage: How big of an exposure can you take as a multiple of your initial deposit. A 50x leverage means you can trade a value worth $5,000 with an initial deposit of $100.

Now that we know these basic terms and ideas, let's dive into the 6 best FX pairs you can trade.

EUR/USD

EUR/USD is the most liquid currency pair. The Euro is the official currency of 19 of the 28 member countries in the Euro-zone. Because of this pair's popularity, you will see huge amounts of data available for analysis. Its low volatility also makes it your best trading candidate. The Euro is known as the "anti-dollar," which means these two have an inverse relationship.

USD/JPY

USD/JPY is the second most traded currency pair due. This is largely due to extreme intervention by the Japanese Central Bank to stabilize the value of its currency. This pair has very low volatility, low spreads, and plentiful data available for analysis. The pair is also favorable to many carry traders.

GBP/USD

GBP/USD is the third most commonly traded currency pair by volume, with Sterling (GBP) serving as the official currency of the United Kingdom. Analytical data is readily available for this pair. But unlike the previous two pairs, GBP/USD is more volatile, and is weighed by political factors affecting the United Kingdom. Due to its high volatility it also has higher spreads, making the pair riskier than the other two currency pairs. However, this high risk also presents opportunities for higher profits for traders who understand the pair's dynamics.

AUD/USD

Also known as the Aussie, the AUD is Australia's national currency. AUD/USD is the fourth largest currency pair in terms of trading volume. This pair is more volatile than the other pairs we have discussed due to Australia's dependence on highly volatile commodity exports (primarily coal and iron ore). You can achieve huge profits from this pair if you understand the movements in commodity prices.

USD/CAD

USD/CAD is the fifth most commonly traded pair. One of Canada's major exports is Oil, so the price of oil has a bearing on the price of this pair. Higher oil prices tend to help strengthen the CAD. An oil analyst and a currency trader could be a deadly combination for trading profitably in this pair. You can find plenty of useful data for this pair as well.

USD/CHF

The sixth largest traded currency, USD/CHF is popular due to Switzerland's safe haven status driven by its political and financial stability, as well as 80% being correlated with gold. Traders flock to sell this pair in highly uncertain environments to safeguard themselves. This pair has withstood the test of time and survived the Great Recession of 2008, when it appreciated against all major currencies except the Japanese Yen.

TAKEAWAY

There are several differences between the many currency pairs, but your best trading pair in the FX market is the pair you know inside out. Essentially, you should have an expert knowledge about the economy, its indicators, and political developments in the country. It could be your home currency, even if it is not trade as actively traded as the pairs mentioned earlier. If you have a good grasp on political and economic developments of more than one country, you are more likely to trade them all profitably. As a currency trader, you should maintain an economic calendar to be prepared for the data events in advance. You should also use leverage responsibly to avoid getting washed out if few of your trades go horribly wrong.

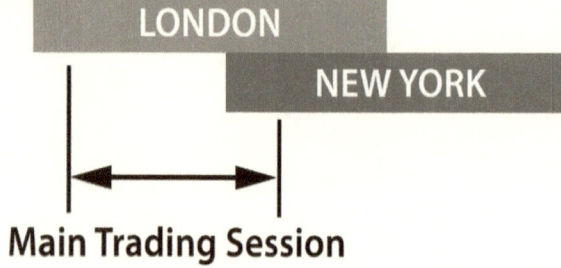

Main Trading Session

BEST TIMES TO TRADE FOREX

—— ·▮— ▮ —▮· ——

One of the biggest lures of Forex trading for newbies is the Forex market's 24-hours-a-day-five-days-a-week trading availability. However, seasoned Forex traders know that not all times are right for trading. As a trader, you need to figure out which time suits you the best based on your geographical location and your preferred currency pair.

GLOBAL MARKET TRADING HOURS

To understand and determine which time suits you best, let's take a look at market timings for the major Forex trading markets around the world. (all times shown in Eastern Standard Time or EST):

London: 3am to 11am

New York: 8am to 5pm

Sydney: 5pm to 2am

Tokyo: 7pm to 4am

Together, London and New York account for over 50% of the worldwide Forex trades, and London alone accounts for over 37% of the Forex market activity. After these two markets, Tokyo is the next highest in trade volume. Therefore, any time the London exchange is open would be a good time to trade. However, the most optimal time to trade that session would during the London and New York trading hours.

WHY TRADE THE OVERLAP?

Each exchange in the Forex market trades independently in its key currency pairs. The pairs will be relatively liquid during their market hours, and even more so when the two currency markets overlap. As mentioned above, the most common best time for traders based in London and New York is the four-hour overlap (8 a.m. to 12 noon) of those two markets.

Even if you are based in other countries, but your trading interest is major currencies like USD, EUR, JPY and GBP, the optimum time to trade will be the overlap of the London and New York trading hours.

EXCEPTIONAL VOLATILITY

Apart from these overlaps, the Forex market shows significant trading activity during major news breaks, and volatility increases exceptionally in times of unexpected good or bad news. This can happen regardless of the timing and open markets. Therefore, as a trader you must keep your calendars updated on major announcements and their expected timings, to ensure you trade effectively and profitably.

WHEN NOT TO TRADE

Knowing when NOT to trade is just as important as knowing when to trade. There are some times when it is more beneficial to NOT trade:

Times of Chaos: Chaotic events, such as an outbreak of war or a disease, are prime examples of when you should refrain from trading. Markets will act irrationally longer than you can remain solvent, as they say. During times of chaos, normal trading will not take place and price behavior will not make analytical sense.

After a huge loss: A huge loss can be very painful. Trust me, I know from experience. This pain is what I could imagine a heart attack feels like. This type of feeling puts your trading at risk, so be sure to wait until you are calm, cool, and collected, before you begin trading again. This is absolutely crucial. Otherwise, you risk making irrational decisions to try and cover your losses, which never puts you in a good situation. It's best to simply take a break until you can calm your emotions and think logically.

During an Election: I would recommend holding off on trading during elections, as implied volatility will be through the roof. Of course you can make money from the volatility, but the goal here is to avoid the irrational market altogether.

It can be hard to hold off, but it will keep you in the game. Use this time to study and perfect your skills.

WHAT MOVES THE FOREX MARKET?

In general, market moves are determined by the supply and demand of that market's constituents. In Forex markets, these constituents are currencies of different countries. Higher demand or lower supply of one currency against another currency therefore leads to a higher price for the former. Supply and demand for currencies is impacted by many factors, but they can be grouped into two main categories, macroeconomic factors and geopolitical factors, which we will discuss in detail.

MACROECONOMIC FACTORS

Macroeconomics often dictates major movements in the Forex markets. An economy's overall strength is gauged by indicators such as economic growth, inflation, employment and wage levels, interest rate movements, central bank actions, and trade and capital flows. These are widely tracked, high frequency indicators released by authorities on specified dates. Each of these

macroeconomic factors impacts the markets in unique ways, so let's take a closer look at each of them.

ECONOMIC GROWTH, INFLATION, AND OTHER HIGH FREQUENCY DATA

Market experts and economists forecast and estimate these data points before they are officially published. Because traders price currencies based on those forecasts, surprise discrepancies between the forecasts and actual data often result in significant market movements, both positive and negative. A positive surprise leads to higher demand for the local currency due to capital influx. This increased demand then pushes the local currency prices higher in comparison to other currencies. Conversely, a negative surprise does just the opposite and pulls prices down.

Currencies also respond to economic policies. For example, a forthcoming capitalist economy may have a rising currency, while a closed, opaque economy may experience a declining currency, assuming all other factors remain the same.

Forex Traders track economic data closely and keep a calendar to plan their trades around the release of this data.

INTEREST RATE MOVEMENTS

According to basic economic principles, higher interest rates attract more capital to an economy. As a forex trader, this means that you should be on

the lookout for signs of growth and inflation. This will ultimately determine the direction of an economy's interest rates. Large amounts of money will follow countries with high interest rates, pushing the value of its currency higher compared to other currencies.

CENTRAL BANK ACTIONS

Central Banks also intervene in the Forex markets through both direct and indirect measures. An example of a direct measure is buying and selling currencies to counter excess volatility. Indirect measures include loosening capital flow restrictions or releasing liquidity in the markets.

EXTERNAL TRADE AND BALANCE OF PAYMENTS

A currency's demand also depends on its trade balance with the external world. If the country is a net exporter, it will typically have a strengthening currency (assuming everything else remains the same). This is because traders will buy the country's currency to pay for their merchandise, leading to increased demand and a higher value.

A country's currency will also experience high demand if it is a popular investment destination that attracts significant short-term and long-term capital flows. Countries with high trade deficits can also experience rising currencies if they attract large capital flows.

FLIGHT TO SAFETY

When economies face extraordinarily turbulent times, investors and traders often move their capital to safer countries like the United States and other developed countries. This weakening of riskier, vulnerable currencies such as the AUD and NZD leads traders to flock to safe haven currencies such as the CHF, JPY, and USD. This usually causes the unwinding of many carry trades and can lead to significant price movements.

GEOPOLITICAL FACTORS

While major Forex movements can happen due to macroeconomic factors, geopolitics also contributes its share of influence. Countries marred by political uncertainties will often have dwindling currencies that can lose much of their value as traders lose confidence in the currency. This can also happen to countries on the brink of war or fighting insurgencies and dictatorships.

NATURAL DISASTERS

Natural disasters represent a black swan event for many people. They can happen at any time and are extremely difficult to prepare for, even for stable, developed countries. Commodity prices tend to see huge swings when events such as these occur, so keep an eye on countries that are large exporters of goods and have been affected by a tragedy.

CONCLUSION

Most Forex traders spend a good share of their time analyzing macro data and trading according to their individual strategies. Some smart traders only look for extraordinary events (like Brexit or the financial crisis) to find prime opportunities trade Forex. Forex market movements can be better understood by observing the macro data and reactions by market participants after the release of economic data. A detailed analysis of historical data can provide useful insights when developing a strategy. The Forex market is extremely dynamic, and traders must constantly remain on their toes to respond not only to the discussed factors, but also to a host of other factors. Learning to deal with uncertainty is of utmost importance if you want to be a successful Forex trader.

HOW CURRENCIES
CORRELATE WITH OIL

Correlation between currency and oil can be based on multiple factors such as the resource richness of a country, its trade balance, and market sentiment. Currencies of countries that are rich in oil and oil resources tend to have a highly positive correlation with oil prices. Conversely, currencies of countries that are net importers of oil tend to carry a negative correlation with oil prices.

OIL AND THE USD

Until the shale revolution in 2005, the United States was a large importer of crude oil. The shale revolution dramatically increased oil production in the U.S., thereby leading to reduced dependence on oil imports from other countries.

Prior to this dramatic uplift, the USD was negatively correlated with oil prices. Now that the country is self-sufficient in terms of oil, the correlation has turned slightly positive. However, the currency is still not as positively correlated with oil prices as other currencies, such as the CAD. This is because the U.S. is not a significant exporter of the commodity and has more diverse sources of economic activity.

The USD showed an extreme inverse relationship with the oil price after 2014 when crude oil prices experienced a significant decline from $100+ to the high $20s. The dollar strengthened during this time because the U.S. economy saw strong growth while keeping its finances intact. The U.S., however, ceased to be an importer of oil in 2011, making this inverse relation attributable to many other factors outside the oil price decline. During this time, trading the USD would have been beneficial and profitable for traders.

The U.S., however, holds the potential to become a petrocurrency if the shale boom further solidifies the country's position in international oil trade, making it a prominent exporter. If that occurs, the USD will be strongly positively correlated with oil prices.

OIL AND ITS PRODUCERS

The currencies of major oil producing countries like Saudi Arabia, Russia, Canada, and Brazil all have a high positive correlation with crude prices since their economic activity and exports is significantly dependent on oil. These countries reaped tremendous benefits from 1998 to 2008, when WTI crude jumped from the high teens to over $160, helping them create excesses in their respective economies. This boom fueled the belief that the bull run would continue forever.

Unfortunately, these currencies have suffered heavily as WTI Crude oil prices dropped from over $100 in 2014 to the high 30's in 2016, the effects of which are still visible throughout their economies.

The excessive volatility in crude prices have had an awakening impact on these countries, pushing them to de-risk their economies from the wild swings in oil prices. The continuing structural shift away from polluting fuels toward environmentally-friendly alternatives also poses a threat to their economies, unless they work to counter the negative effects.

Until these countries find solutions to their problem of overreliance on oil, their currencies will continue to have highly positive correlations with oil.

OIL AND SENTIMENT

Oil price has had a sentimental impact on other commodity prices and currencies that is driven by a fear of deflation. The downward oil price spiral seen after 2014 led to a collapse in other commodity prices as well. It also led to dwindling confidence in countries with little or no oil resources, like the Euro Zone and countries rich in mining resources like Australia. To restore confidence, the ECB resorted to quantitative Easing (QE), which in turn helped support the Euro.

SUMMARY

Though all the factors we have discussed define the correlation between oil and currencies, this correlation is extremely straightforward for currencies of major oil producers, exporters, and importers. If everything else remains the same, a large exporter will have a positive correlation with oil prices and a large importer will have a negative correlation with oil prices. The correlation is extremely tricky, however, for countries that are self dependent on oil. Forex traders typically perform the best when they choose the former set of currencies and avoid the latter.

"Nearly all of our existing power sources are generators which use a heat cycle. This includes our coal, oil, and gas fired utilities, our automobiles, trucks, and trains, and even our nuclear fission utility power plants"

– Wilson Greatbatch

HOW CURRENCIES
CORRELATE WITH GOLD

————— • ▎ — ▌ — ▎ • —————

This shiny yellow metal is considered to be a safe haven, and investors flock to it in times of uncertainty. Therefore, most currencies have a negative correlation with gold, unless an economy is dependent on gold prices, as is the case for the CHF.

CURRENCY CORRELATION

Correlation can be helpful in formulating your Forex trading strategy. It is good to understand the gold's correlation with currencies and how the relationship has changed over periods of time. That knowledge can help you understand trends and determine the right currency pair to trade.

For example, the USD has for a long time displayed a negative correlation with gold prices, while the CHF and AUD have shown a positive correlation.

Let's take a closer look at why this is the case.

GOLD AND USD

Gold and USD currently have an inverse relationship. When the USD declines, people look for alternatives to safeguard the value of their money, this is when they flock to gold. Even though the US Dollar is considered to be a safe asset, gold is considered to be even safer. In times of extreme uncertainty, money is often moved from currencies (including USD) to gold.

GOLD AND AUD

Australia is a large producer and exporter of gold, which is why its currency is positively related to the precious metal. When gold prices rise, Australia gets paid more for its gold and, as a result, demand for the Aussie increases. Here, traders should trade the AUD/USD pair due to its correlation with gold.

GOLD AND CHF

Switzerland has one of the largest gold reserves in the world. The Swiss Franc is also considered to be a safe asset due to the strong Swiss economy and its conservative governance. Since the country maintains a large part of its reserves in gold (about 80%), it tends to have a positive correlation with gold since the reserves increase in value when gold prices go up.
The best way to trade this correlation is through USD/CHF, which tends to have a negative correlation with gold.

SUMMARY

Because of its safe haven status, gold generally has an inverse relation with major currencies. In a risk averse environment, currencies are sold to buy gold, with the opposite happening when people are willing to take risks. However, this relation does not hold for AUD and CHF as demonstrated by empirical evidence and logical conclusions.

The economics and correlation, however, are not sacrosanct. These relationships do change and traders should be well versed in the factors that can drive change. It is important to note that every situation should be viewed differently, but be sure to keep the correlation basics in mind. For example, say there is a case where the USD and gold both are appreciating, led by problems in some part of the world that does not impact the U.S. Here, both the USD and gold are considered safe assets and appreciate simultaneously, displaying positive correlation.In cases such as this, you will need to read between the lines to understand exactly what is happening.

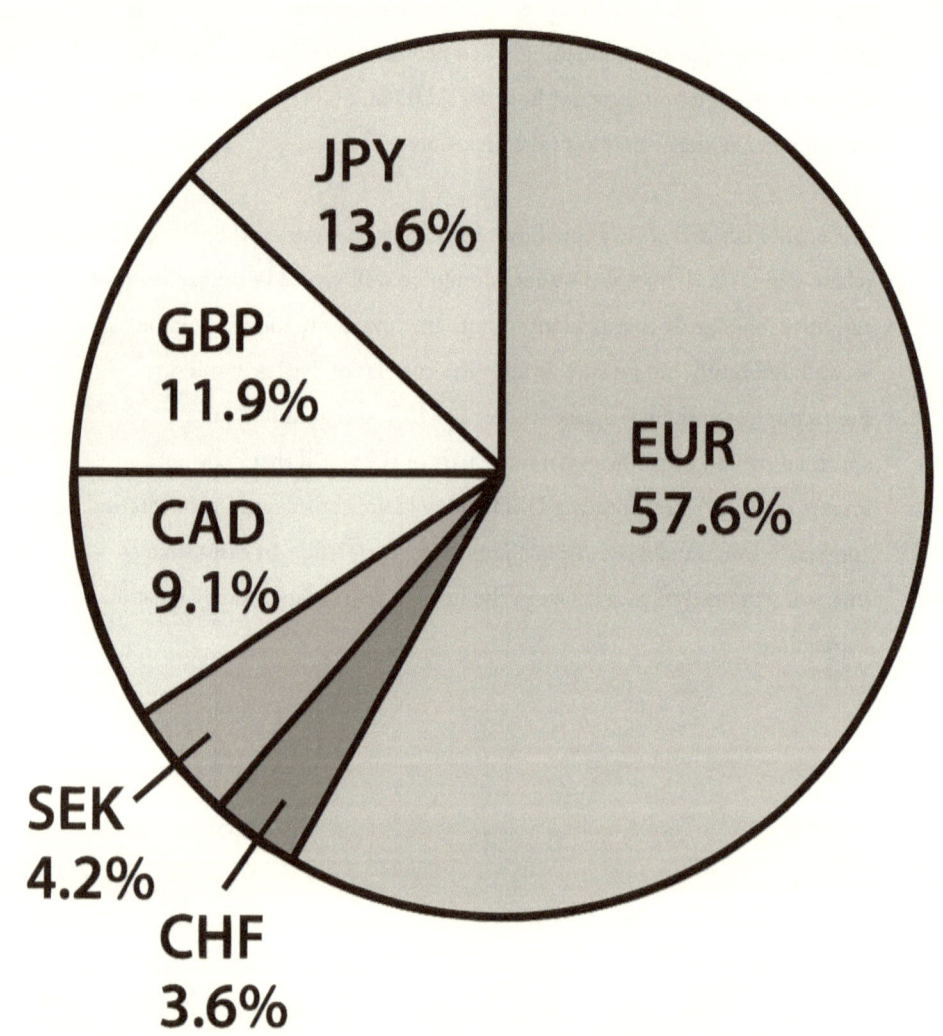

THE U.S. DOLLAR INDEX (USDX)

———— • ▮ — ▮ — ▮ • ————

The USDX, or U.S. Dollar Index, is an index measuring the value of the U.S. Dollar relative to the value of a basket of currencies of six major trading partners of the United States.

CONSTITUENTS OF THE USDX

The index currently consists of the exchange rates of the Euro (EUR), Japanese Yen (JPY), Canadian Dollar (CAD), British Pound (GBP), Swedish Krona (SEK) and Swiss Franc (CHF).

The index works just like any other index, with each constituent carrying a defined weight. The index as a whole is calculated based on the geometric weighted average of the exchange rates of the constituent currencies with respect to the USD.

Below are the weights of the six currencies included in the USDX:

EUR 57.6%

JPY 13.6%

GBP 11.9%

CAD 9.1%

SEK 4.2%

CHF 3.6%

The Euro has the highest weight in the index as the 19 member countries that use the Euro are the United States' biggest trading partners.

HISTORY OF USDX

The USDX started in 1973 with a base of 100. Since then, its value has been measured relative to this base. It was formed after the dissolution of the Bretton Woods Agreement, when the member governments chose to let their currencies float relative to other currencies.

The index was changed in 1999 when the Euro was introduced and replaced currencies of several European countries. However, the index hasn't kept pace with the altered trade picture of the U.S., in which China, South Korea, and Mexico have become much bigger trading partners than countries such as Sweden and Switzerland.

The index has seen wild long-term swings, with it touching a high of 164.72 in February 1985 and a low of 70.698 at the height of the subprime crisis. As of November 2019, the index was trading at 98.03.

INTERPRETING THE USDX

An increasing USDX value denotes an appreciating USD and a declining basket of its constituent currencies, at least in relation to the USD. A declining USDX value means the opposite.

You should note that any percentage change in the USDX does not mean the basket currencies have changed in the opposite direction by the exact percentage. The exact percentage change in the basket can be calculated using the following formula:

Change in the Basket of Currencies = 1 - 1/ (1+ % change in USD).

This change will always be directionally opposite to the initial change in the USDX.

For example, if the USDX changed by +10% in a year, the basket currencies would have changed by -9.1% (1 - 1/(1+0.1).

TRADING THE USDX

Financial products (futures and options) based on USDX are traded on the Intercontinental Exchange. They can also be bought indirectly using exchange traded funds (ETFs) and mutual funds.

WHEN TO TAKE PROFITS
OR PLACE A TRADE

Most traders want to know where to place their trade or where to take a profit. The answer is pretty simple actually: Support or Resistance levels. A price is usually doing one of two things (excluding times of chaos):

- trending between past price levels
- reaching new highs or lows

Once you have found your chart pattern, it is up to you as a strategic trader to place your stop and limit order, one that has a very good risk / reward ratio. I like to shoot for a 1:3 or 1:4 ratio. How far out the level is, that is up to you. The farther you let it ride, the more profit potential you have, along with more risk as well. On the other hand, a closer support level means less risk, but a reduced chance of profitability.

There is no real way to predict a given market, so you need to try to find indications of what the market is doing. There is also no way to predict the full extent of the trend, so you have to take what the markets give you. Focusing on the near term is very important.

Remember:
- It is more important to keep your trading size down than to pin-point your entry and exit
- Focus on the present and what's happening now
- During volatile markets, use wider stops with lower leverage
- Never act on impulses

"You don't have to be great to get started, but you have to get started to be great"

- Les Brown

TOOLS FOR FINDING
TRADING LEVELS

—— • ı — ▌ — ı • ——

There are a few tools that tend to be very helpful to traders. As stated in the beginning, you don't want to over crowd your mind with too much news or too many indicators. The best traders keep things simple. The following tools are simple and easy to use.

MOVING AVERAGES

Moving averages can either be simple or exponential. In a simple moving average, all the prices in the average carry the same weight, meaning that it moves relatively slow. In an exponential moving average, the more recent period prices carry a higher weight, providing a recency to the average that makes it more reflective of the current price move. We will go over these again later in the book.

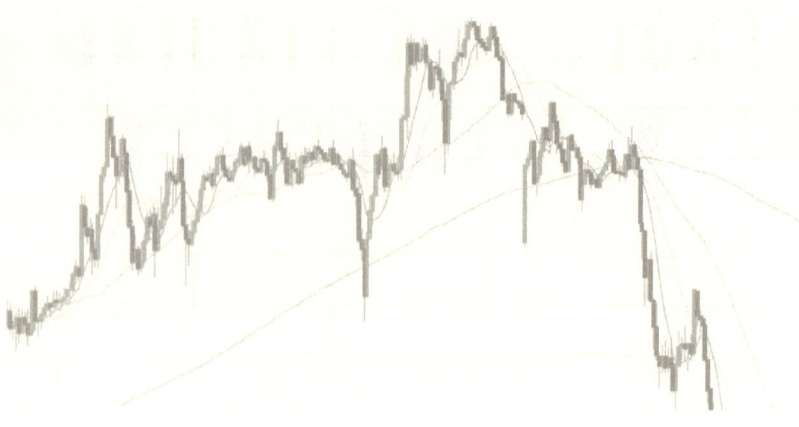

SUPPORT AND RESISTANCE

Support and Resistance are buying and selling zones, respectively, that traders use as psychological levels where demand and supply for the asset changes. Price action traders draw support and resistance lines on charts. They use these charts to trade accordingly when price reaches any of these zones.

BOLLINGER BANDS

Bollinger bands have been known to be very helpful to price action traders. Here, the idea is to find a chart where the price has "broken" through the bands. Breakouts such as the one shown in the picture below can be very profitable because the trend usually follows in the direction of the breakout.

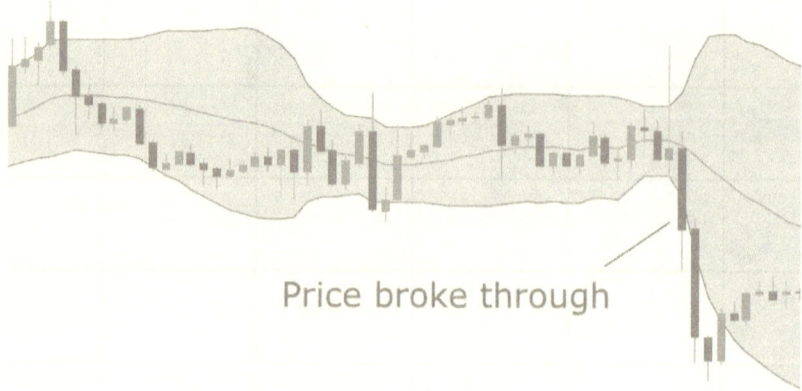

Price broke through

FIBONACCI

According to the Fibonacci system, a strongly trending stock is believed to go through a pullback, which will amount to one of the percentages in the Fibonacci Retracement Tool. These pullback retracements are 23.6%, 38.2%, 61.8% or 76.4%. The 50% retracement level, which is not a part of the original number series, is also considered to be an important retracement level in technical analysis.

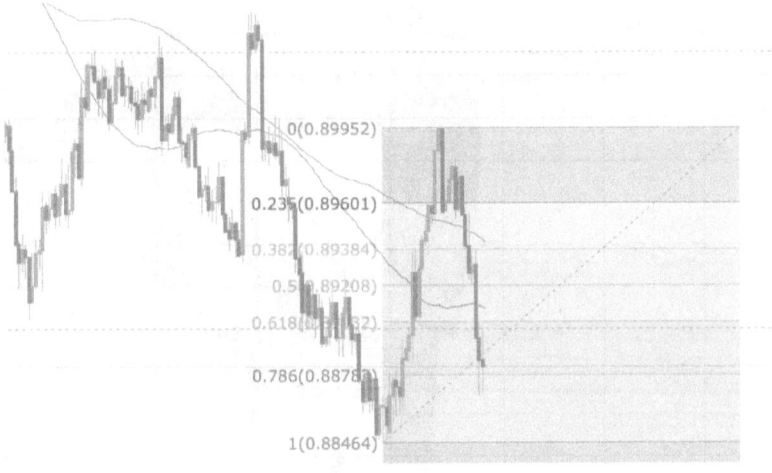

In the image above, price proceeded all the way to the 0.786 level, where we can see that sellers are having a difficult time pushing through.

CANDLESTICKS

———— • —**|**— • ————

Most traders want to know where to place their trade or where to take a profit. The answer is pretty simple actually: Support or Resistance levels. A price is usually doing one of two things (excluding times of chaos):

- trending between past price levels
- reaching new highs or lows

Once you have found your chart pattern, it is up to you as a strategic trader to place your stop and limit order, one that has a very good risk / reward ratio. I like to shoot for a 1:3 or 1:4 ratio. How far out the level is, that is up to you. The farther you let it ride, the more profit potential you have, along with more risk as well. On the other hand, a closer support level means less risk, but a reduced chance of profitability.

There is no real way to predict a given market, so you need to try to find indications of what the market is doing. There is also no way to predict

BULLISH CANDLE PATTERNS

HAMMER

- Bullish reversal candle
- Opposite of a shooting star
- Gets its name from its hammer shape, with a long wick followed by a small body

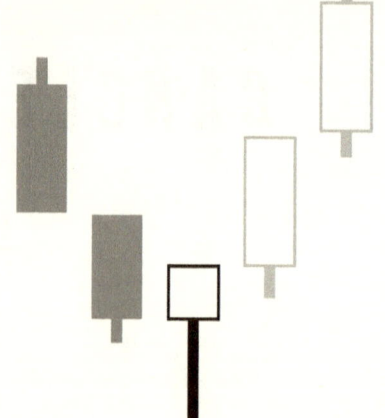

INVERTED HAMMER

- Bullish signal found at the bottom of a downtrend
- Reversal signal to the upside
- Gets its name from its hammer shape
- Small body, long upper wick, little or no bottom wick

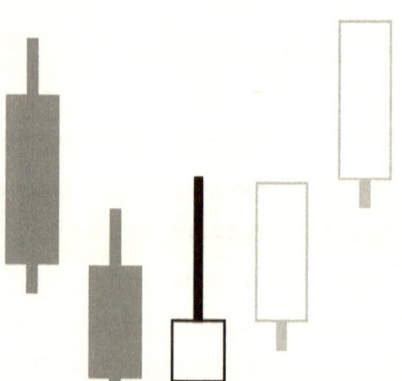

DRAGONFLY DOJI

- Occurs during a downtrend
- Indicates buyers are becoming more dominant
- Occurs when sellers are able to push prices downwards, but support is found and pushes it back to the open

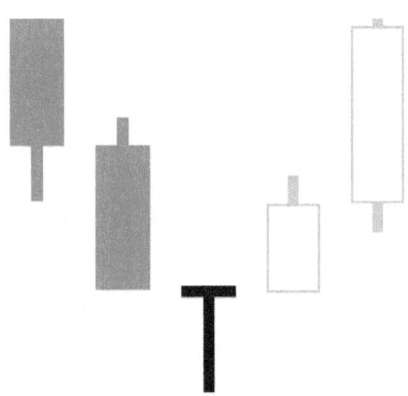

BULLISH ENGULFING

- Shows strong buying pressure
- Usually appears at the bottom of downtrend
- Opens at or below the previous candle's close
- Body then engulfs the previous candle and closes above its open

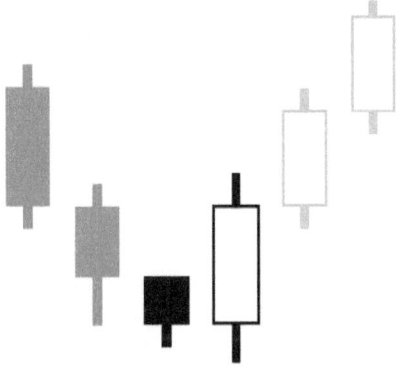

PIERCING LINE

- Demonstrates a high level of sellers, but buyers are gaining control
- Found at the bottom of a downtrend
- Tends to gap up at times due to high volatility

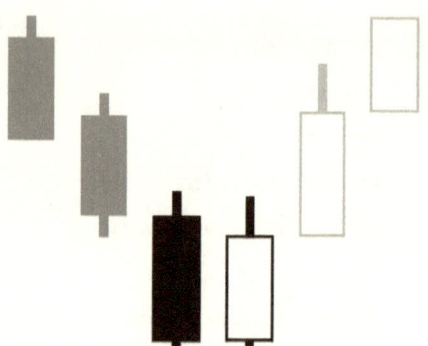

MORNING STAR

- Opposite of the Evening star
- Forms after a downtrend
- Indicates a reversal could be near
- Warns of weakness in a downtrend

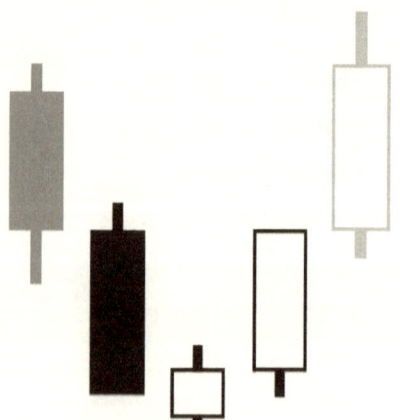

SHOOTING STAR

- Bearish reversal pattern
- Has a wick at least half the candle length
- Shows that sellers have taken control and pushed the price down

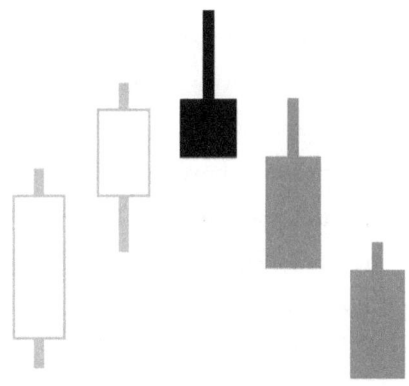

HANGING MAN

- Indicates an increase in selling pressure during an uptrend
- Looks like a hammer, but the wick continues briefly past the body
- Poses a threat to the downside

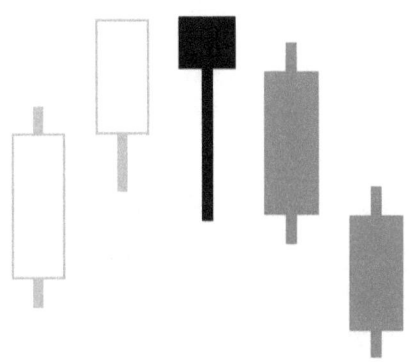

GRAVESTONE DOJI

- Formed when the open, low, and closing price share the same values, with a long upper shadow
- Occurs when buyers are able to push prices upwards, but resistance pushes it back to the open

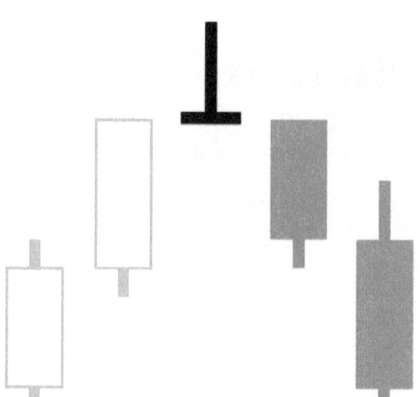

BEARISH ENGULFING

- Shows strong selling pressure
- Opens at or above the previous candle's
- close
- Body engulfs the previous candle and closes below its open

DARK CLOUD COVER

- Bearish reversal pattern
- Piercing lines through candle after an uptrend
- Appears in an uptrend
- Signals potential weakness and that sellers could gain control

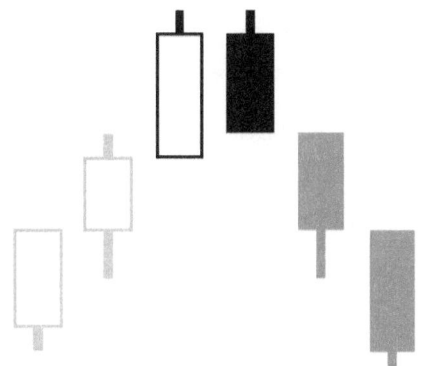

EVENING STAR

- Opposite of a morning star
- Reversal pattern found at the top of an uptrend
- A strong indicator is if the volume on the 3rd
- candle (the bearish candle) is greater than the volume on the first

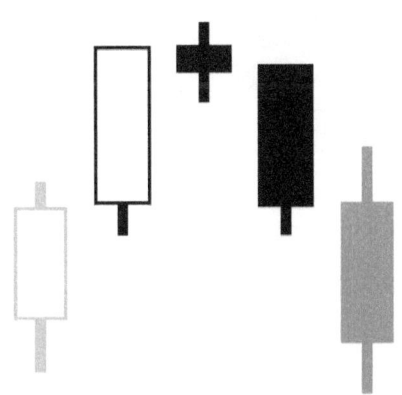

DOJI

- Shows indecision between buyers and sellers
- Has the same open and close price
- If formed after a series of hollow candles, it could indicate that whoever is in control is losing strength

SPINNING TOP

- Similar to a doji
- Formation bearing another indecision
- Could be sign of a reversal if formed after a large move up or down

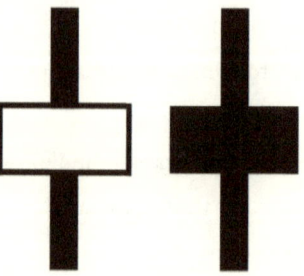

CHART PATTERNS

---·ı–❚–ı·---

"Do not anticipate and move without market confirmation. Being a little late in your trade is your insurance that you are right or wrong"

Jesse Livermore

CONTINUATION PATTERNS

FLAGS

Flags get their name from their appearance, and are a result of tight sideways price action amid a strong trend in the price. It can be constructed using two parallel trend lines that look like a flag when seen on the chart after a large spike in price. Volume generally declines during the flag formation, which is often followed by breakouts.

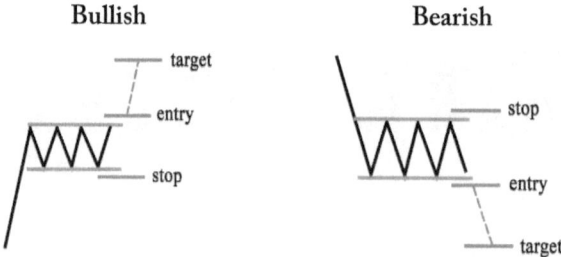

PENNANTS

A Pennant is a consolidation pattern formed by a sharp increase in price, thereby creating a flagpole shaped candle. It then has a period of consolidation that usually breaks out in the direction of the trend. Like flags, a Pennant is also accompanied by declining volumes.

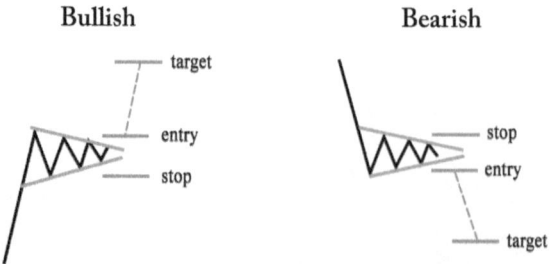

RISING AND FALLING WEDGES

There are two types of wedges, rising and falling. A rising wedge signals a bearish reversal pattern and a falling wedge signals a bullish reversal could be forming. These shapes have been known to have a high probability.

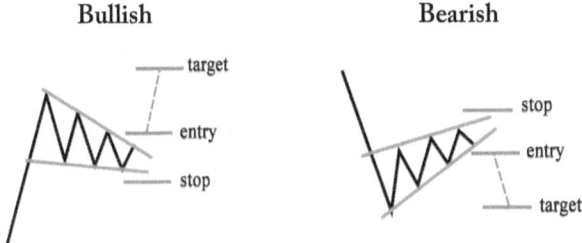

CUP AND HANDLE

A cup and handle is a powerful pattern formed in an uptrend, signifying that the uptrend would resume once the formation is complete. The pattern looks like a cup on the left with a small handle on the side. An Inverse-Cup and handle would be identical to this, but upside down. The cup part of the pattern is a "U" shape pattern while the handle part is more of a wedge or pennant. Below is a chart demonstrating a cup and handle pattern.

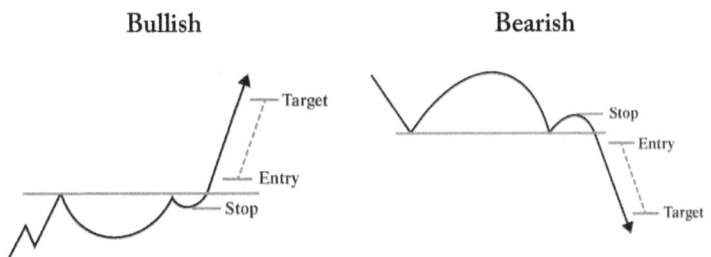

TRIANGLES

Another pattern that has high probability is the Triangle. Triangles are prolonged consolidation patterns that result in either a breakdown or breakout depending on the kind of triangle formation. There are three types of triangle formations: symmetrical, ascending or descending.

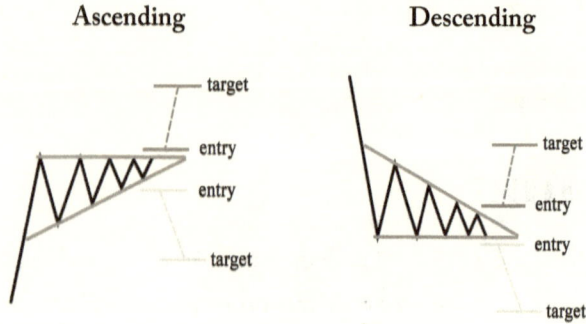

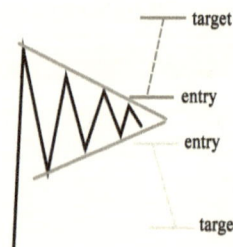

HEAD AND SHOULDERS

Head and shoulders patterns appear at the end of any trend. This pattern resembles a head and shoulder, with the first shoulder formed in the direction of the trend followed by a price reversal. The price again comes back up and surpasses the earlier shoulder level and touches a new high/low, forming the head, before coming back again. The price again moves up/down, forming the second shoulder while coming back again, marking the reversal of the trend.

In a head and shoulder pattern, the price is not able to break new highs/lows after three attempts, signifying the reversal of the ongoing trend.

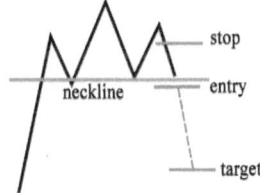

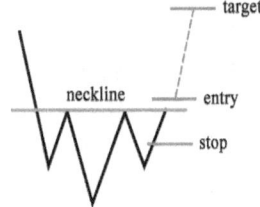

DOUBLE TOP AND BOTTOMS

Similar to head and shoulders patterns, double tops and bottoms are formed at the end of the uptrend and downtrend, respectively, signifying two failed attempts by the price to breach earlier highs/lows. Volatility increases during this pattern formation, indicating that the torchbearers of the trend (bulls or bears) are losing their breath.

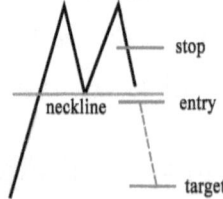 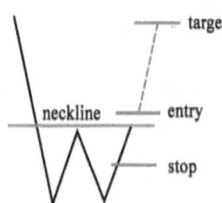

TRIPLE TOP AND BOTTOM

One of the most powerful chart patterns is the triple top or bottom. This pattern signifies three futile attempts to reach a new high, often leading to reversals. In the event that it does break past the support or resistance level, it could very well reach new highs or lows

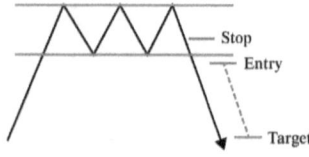 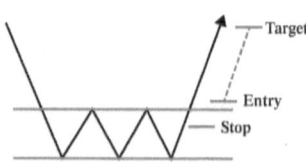

SUMMARY

Like any other trading technique or strategy, price action trading also has its share of hits and misses. It requires an optimum level of risk taking and risk management. You will undoubtedly experience false breakouts, unidentifiable patterns, and many other negative surprises that will make your job as a trader difficult. While a losing trade cannot be avoided, the goal is to manage these effectively. Every trading strategy should have strong stop-loss rules. You won't be right all the time in this business; therefore, your mission is to set a plan and stick to it, otherwise you will incur losses.

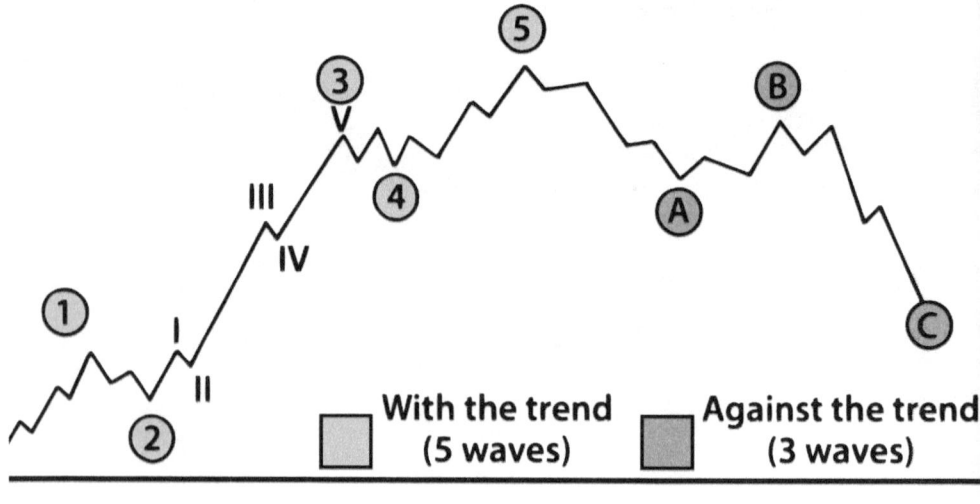

ELLIOTT WAVE THEORY

Developed by Ralph Nelson Elliott in the 1930s and popularized by Robert Prechter in 1970s, the Elliott wave theory emphasises that markets demonstrate the same type of long-term and short-term patterns, which Elliot described as fractal wave patterns.

According to Elliot, such patterns not only apply to financial markets, but also to other situations in which many people come together and act simultaneously. Examples of this include situations like buying homes or taking out loans.

A BRIEF HISTORY

The theory was first developed by Ralph Nelson Elliott in the 1930s. Elliot came up with the theory after meticulously studying index movements dating back 75 years. His detailed study included analyzing yearly, monthly, weekly, daily, and self-made hourly and 30-minute charts.

After studying the data, Elliot specified rules on identifying, predicting, and capitalizing on the wave patterns formed by the markets. He also noted that these patterns cannot predict exact future price movements, but they can be helpful in figuring out future market corrections. These patterns, when used alongside other indicators, can provide useful insights on the current state of the market. As such, they can also help you cash in on specific opportunities.

All of Elliot's work is covered in "R.N. Elliott's Masterworks," that was published in 1994.

THE THEORY

The theory basically states that crowd psychology works in certain patterns, which repeat themselves over time. Financial markets also follow these patterns because they are places where large flocks of people with differing views come together to trade.

The theory also states that the price movements are predictable because they tend to follow the same repeating wave pattern. These waves are called motive waves and corrective waves. Together, they form the Elliott Wave pattern.

Now, let's take a closer look at each one.

MOTIVE WAVE - THE FIRST HALF OF ELLIOTT WAVE

A motive wave is a wave that always advances in the direction of the trend of one larger degree. As shown in the following picture, the wave is further subdivided into five smaller sub-waves, three of which – 1,3 and 5 – move in the direction of the larger trend (up) and are called actionary sub-waves. The other two – 2 and 4 – move in the direction opposite to the larger trend (down) and are called corrective sub-waves. The following picture depicts the application of the theory when the larger trend is an uptrend. Its application remains the same when the larger trend is a downtrend.

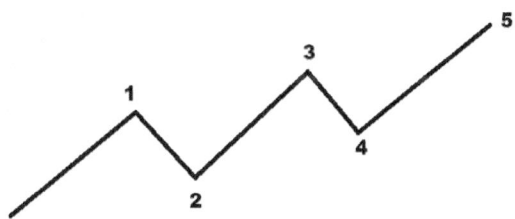

There are three rules that must be satisfied when considering motive wave formation:

1. Wave 2 always retracts less than 100% of Wave 1.
2. Wave 3 always goes past wave 1 and is longer most of the time.
3. Wave 4 retracts less than wave 3, leading to the final wave 5 to complete the pattern

CORRECTIVE WAVE

A corrective wave is a three sub-wave pattern, as shown in the chart below. It forms after the motive wave and depicts the correction in the larger trend.

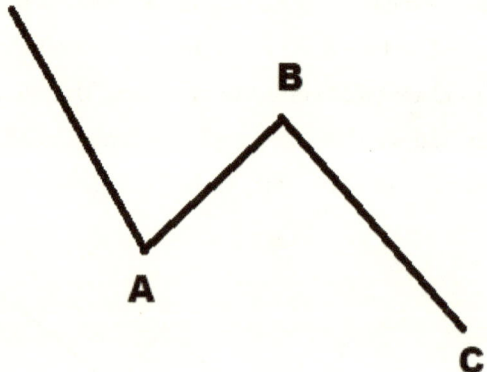

A corrective wave pattern is laid out as a three-wave structure, wherein Waves A and C move in the direction of the trend one higher degree (correction), and Wave B moves in the direction opposite to the direction of higher degree trend.

REMEMBER

Per the theory, this structure is repeated again and again, forming a 5-3-5-3-5 structure. These are very good points that you should become very familiar with, as these will be what you are looking to trade. You want to make sure you ride the wave in the right direction.

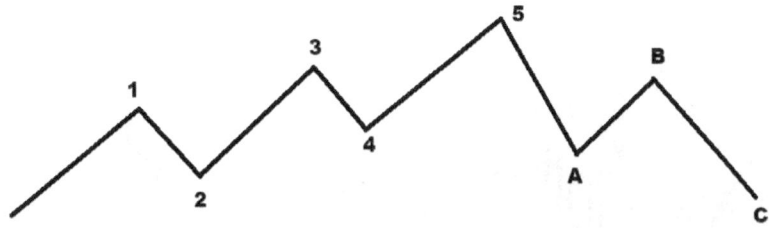

TRADING WITH PRICE ACTION

Trading based on technicals can be confusing because of the many indicators and strategies to follow. It can be both extremely simple and highly complicated at the same time. When starting out, you need something simple and effective to begin your trading. Price action trading is one of the simplest and most effective forms of trading.

The simplicity of price-based trading stems from the fact that the only variable you track is the price. It is real-time rather than lagged, as is the case with many indicator based trading strategies.

WHAT IS PRICE ACTION TRADING?

Price actions trading is trading based solely on the price of an asset. Price action traders rarely use additional indicators to base their trades, and instead look for proven and tested price patterns to initiate and close trades.

A price action trader uses price along with other information like bids, offers, volume, velocity, and magnitude. Traders use tools like trendlines, bollinger bands, and moving averages to frame their price action trading strategies. Using this information, traders identify and wait for price patterns to develop before initiating their trades. Price patterns are useful in identifying the correct entry and exit points.

Price action trading is about understanding the market behavior and psychology. Price behaves a certain way at major points because of the collective market thinking and actions.

Open Buy Position

For example, a common price based trading strategy is buying the stocks at support levels and selling when they approach resistance levels. These levels are nothing but psychological points derived by the trader analyzing the asset's past pricing chart (whole numbers such as 1.1000 or 1.1050 are looked at as psychological support or resistance as well). At a support level, sellers exhaust themselves and buyers take over, while at resistance levels, buyers get exhausted and are taken over by sellers.

COMMON PRICE TRADING STRATEGIES AND PATTERNS

Price action strategies vary based on how the current chart looks. The price may be in an uptrend, in a downtrend, or it may be moving sideways. While trading based on the price, you can use continuation patterns, which will help you trade with the trend. You can also use reversal patterns, which will indicate the reversal of the trend and enable you to trade in the opposite direction.

BREAKOUTS AND BREAKDOWNS

A Breakout or breakdown is a quick advance or decline in the price of an asset after it has been ranging. Normally accompanied by higher volumes, breakouts or breakdowns signal to the trader that the price is witnessing a fresh advance or decline. For example, assume that an asset has traded in range for some time, usually forming a wave like pattern. In the chart below, we see that the price broke through the support and is likely to lead to a reversal.

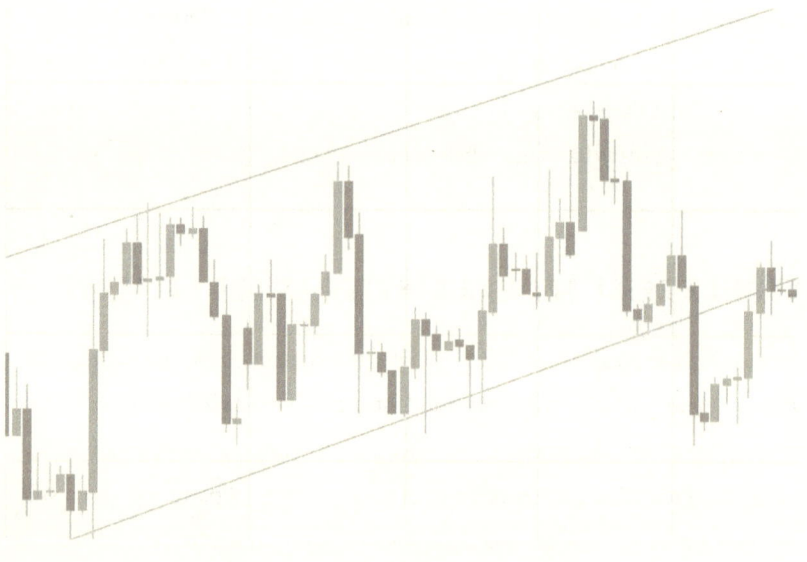

SUPPORT AND RESISTANCE

As stated earlier, support and resistance are buying and selling zones, respectively, that traders use as psychological levels where demand and supply of the asset changes. Price action traders draw support and resistance lines on charts and trade accordingly when price reaches any of these zones.

"Before anything else, preparation is the key to success"

Alexander Graham Bell

TRADING WITH
MOVING AVERAGES

———— • ▪ — ▐ — ▪ • ————

Moving averages are as simple as they sound. In trading, a moving average is the average of the asset's closing price for a specified period. For example, a 10 day moving average is calculated as the average closing price for the last 10 trading days. These moving averages can then be plotted on a chart along with the price to obtain useful trading signals.

In the chart below, we use four Moving Averages. These are the 200 day, the 50 day, 20 day, and 9 day moving averages. As you can see, the farther out the time frame for the moving average, the less of a response you will see in the line.

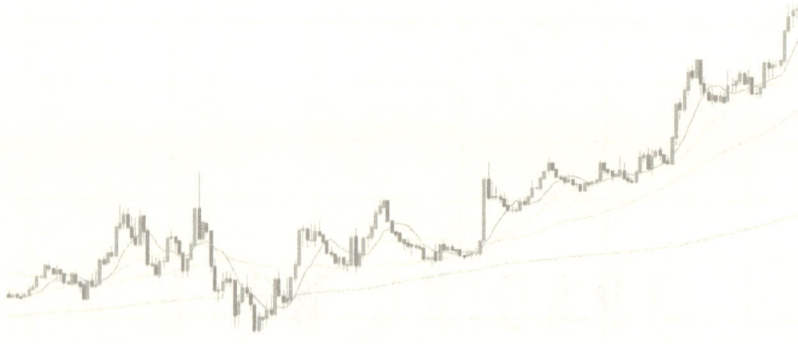

SIGNIFICANCE OF MOVING AVERAGES

The importance of moving average can not be ignored in technical analysis. They are the simplest and one of the most powerful indicators. For starters, moving average tells you the following about the price of an asset:

I. Trend of the Asset price

II. Strength of the Trend

III. The forward momentum and when the momentum is losing steam

IV. Support and Resistance levels

TYPES OF MOVING AVERAGES

Moving averages can either be simple or exponential. In a simple moving average, all prices in the average carry the same weight, meaning it moves somewhat slowly. In an exponential moving average, the more recent period prices carry a higher weight in the average, hence providing a recency to the average and making it more reflective of the current price move.

The rewards of keeping it simple are immense for traders, and those who understand it go a long way. So, let's discuss some of the major strategies that you can use to trade Forex using moving averages.

PRICE AND THE MOVING AVERAGE

The most basic strategy one can use is buying when the price cuts the moving average from one side to the other. The simplicity of this strategy makes it hard to implement, as something that simple is not expected to make any profits. Contrary to this belief, this simple strategy has been extremely helpful in trading. As always, the farther out of the time frame you go, the more reliable the chart will be.

In the chart chart below, the 200 day moving average provided a nice trading opportunity when the price cut the moving average line from below to above. It again provided a shorting opportunity later when the price cut the moving average line from above to below.

Break in the
Moving Averages

Such opportunities are way too common in Forex trading, provided a trader uses them proactively with strict stop losses.

DIFFERING TIME PERIODS MOVING AVERAGE

Another trading strategy you can follow is to implement two or more moving averages with different time periods. For example, you can use a 100-day and 50-day moving average to get useful trading signals. If they cross paths as shown in the chart above, you can find a great trading opportunity.

USING MOVING AVERAGES AS SUPPORT AND RESISTANCE

Moving averages can also be used as support and resistance. Many traders use moving averages as psychological levels to place their trades. To do this successfully, you need to make sure you are trading in the overall direction of the trend.

In an uptrend, the prices see frequent intermittent corrections, which tend to reverse at the moving average levels. In the downtrends, intermittent pull-ups are reversed at the moving average levels.

Moving averages are extremely customizable indicators that provide a trader with great trading signals. History has shown that, despite all the complex trading indicators available to a trader, moving averages do best in terms of simplicity, usability, and effectiveness. With some practice and a good deal of risk management, traders can ace this indicator and trade profitably for long periods of time.

"I learned not to worry so much about the outcome but to concentrate on the step I was on and try to do it as perfectly as I could when I was doing it"
–Steve Wozniak

TRADING WITH THE TREND

———— • ▪ — ▌ — ▪ • ————

Trading with the trend is one of the most profitable trading techniques available, and serves as the backbone of my strategy. In addition to Forex, trading the trend can allow you to make immense profits in other asset classes like equities and commodities as well.

Prices typically tend to move in trend – uptrend or downtrend. At other times, the prices are consolidating or moving within a range. Trend traders, as they are mostly called, use a number of indicators to determine the trend and place their trades at strategic buy or sell points to enter and exit the trades.

Trends can be short-term, medium-term and long-term. Depending on the time-frame in which a trader is trading, they can set the frequency of the charts to determine their trading actions. When doing this, be sure to adjust your level of leverage. The farther out you go on the chart, the less leverage you should use, as it can result in deep losses.

THE TRAITS OF A TREND: TRADING THE HIGH AND LOWS

In technical analysis, an uptrend is characterized by price making higher highs and higher lows with an overall upward direction. Conversely, a downtrend is characterized by lower lows and lower highs with an overall downward direction.

In the picture below, the EUR/USD pair can be clearly seen in an uptrend. The pair continued with higher highs and higher lows with an overall upward direction.

Point of Entry

One simple strategy a trader can implement is buying the stock when it falls in intermittent corrections and ride the upward moves for decent profits. This strategy is also called the "buy the dip" strategy.

The trend would be considered to be reversed when the asset breaks below its last consolidation and begins experiencing lower lows and lower highs.

Alternatively, a stock can be identified to be in a downtrend when it experiences lower lows and lower highs, as shown in the chart below. Here, the trading strategy could be selling short in the intermittent up moves and riding the down moves for decent profits.

Short Position Entry

TRADING BASED ON TREND LINES AND CHANNELS

A more organized way of identifying and trading trends is by using trend lines and channels. A trend line can be drawn connecting two or three initial lows of intermittent corrections in an uptrend and stretching it into the future on the chart to identify the prospective price turning points. With this strategy, the trend line will act as support on where the price should resume the uptrend. Traders will buy when the price nears the trend line, keeping the stop loss slightly below the trend line.

The trend is said to be broken if the price breaks the trend line and declines further, reversing the uptrend. In the picture below, the price bounces back from the trend line at multiple locations before breaking the trend line and reversing the trend.

Open Buy Position

A similar trend line can also be drawn on downtrending stocks, wherein the trend line will be considered as resistance in intermittent upward moves.

Short Position Entry

Channels can also be drawn to ascertain breakout or breakdown zones from consolidation patterns, helping the trader better plan their trades in a more astute manner. In the chart below, the consolidation channel would have helped the trader enter just at the breakout and earn a decent profit from the price move later.

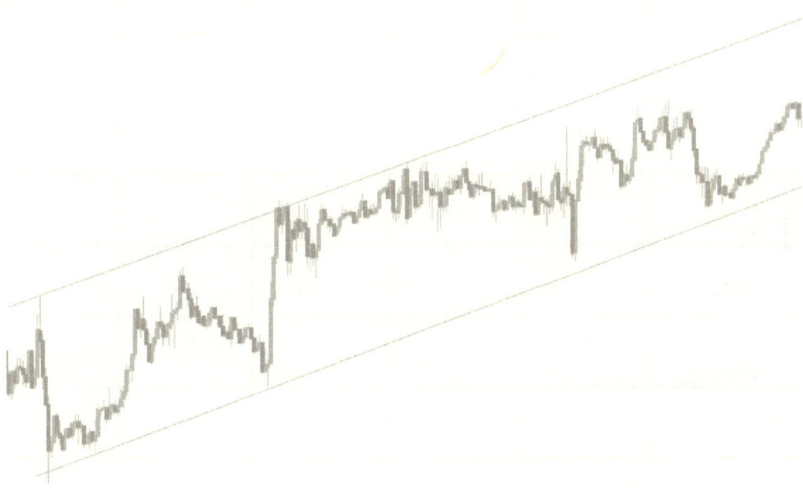

TRADING THE TREND WITH MOVING AVERAGES

Similar to the trend line, moving averages also make the trend identifying and trading process more methodological. The trader simply needs to ensure they use an appropriate moving average length. A smaller moving average will increase the frequency of signals as well as the quantum of false signals. A large, slow moving average will often be too late in signaling. With that said, the length largely depends on the trading time frame of the trader. An intraday trader can use shorter moving averages and still make decent profits, if they get the right strategy and manage risk properly.

The best mid-term moving average could be a 50 period moving average. For daily charts, this means it will show a 50-day moving average; for an hourly chart, it will show a 50 hour moving average. Most people compare this with the 100-day MA.

Moving averages are quite effective in trading continuation patterns. The continuation pattern can be traded in a similar manner as a trend line, meaning the moving average acts as a support for uptrending stocks and resistance for downtrending stocks. Trend reversal happens when the price cuts the moving average and starts trading in the opposite direction.

Short Position Entry

In the above picture, the downtrending price touches the moving average multiple times before reversing the trend. A trader would have earned decent profits shorting the pair at every up move when the price faced resistance around its moving average. The trader would finally have hit a stop loss on the last trade when the prices reversed. Using strategies based on moving averages are a good way to earn profits, and will be discussed in further detail in the next section.

CONCLUSION

With good practice and proper risk management, traders can formulate sustainable trading strategies that result in decent profits in all kinds of markets. The key is to follow strict risk management rules at all times to stay in the game, while trying multiple strategies before you figure out what works for you.

"We may never know where we are going, but we'd better have a good idea where we are"

Howard Marks

TRADING FOREX WITH OPTIONS

—— • ▮ — ▮ — ▮ • ——

Options are one of the most widely traded derivative instruments. Unlike the highly regulated equity and commodity options markets, Forex options are unregulated. Therefore, tradability depends from broker to broker.

Let's start with the basics. Traditional options consist of call and put options, which give the buyer the right but not the obligation to buy or sell a Forex pair at a predetermined price at a specified time in future. An option seller, on the other hand, is obligated to fulfill the trade if the buyer chooses to exercise the right.

WHY USE OPTIONS?

Options are used as a hedge when traders have a large position in the spot market and are fearful about a negative movement in the Forex pair. This is true for large corporations with overseas businesses that earn a large quantum of foreign exchange.

Options are also popular as a speculating medium due to their low risk and high reward characteristics for traders who want to go long. Just as in the spot markets, traders can also participate in options markets to profit from short term market movements.

OPTIONS PRICING

The price of an option is based on the current market price, the strike price of the option, its time to expiration, and implied volatility. Time value decays as the option approaches the expiry date.

CALL OPTIONS

Call options increase in value when the price of the security increases, and decrease in value when the price decreases.

RIGHT OR OBLIGATION?

Buyer: This gives the buyer the *right* to buy the option contract at the call's strike price at or before the expiration.

Seller: This gives the seller the *obligation* to sell the option contract at the call's strike price, if it is assigned.

CALLS ARE PROFITABLE WHEN:

Buyer: The price of the call is trading at a higher price than the initial purchase price.

Seller: The price of the call is trading lower than the original sale price.

PUT OPTIONS

Put options increase in value when the price of the security decreases, and decrease in value when the price increases.

RIGHT OR OBLIGATION?

Buyer: This gives the buyer the *right* to sell the option contract at the put's strike price or before expiration.

Seller: This gives the seller the *obligation* to buy the option contract at the put's strike price, if assigned.

PUTS ARE PROFITABLE WHEN:

Buyer: The price of the put is higher than the original purchase price.

Seller: The price of the put is lower than the original sale price.

OPTION EXAMPLE:

Say we have an American EUR/USD call option to buy EUR 100,000 available with the right to buy the pair at or before 31 March at a strike price of 1.1000. In this case, if the pair moves above the strike price of 1.1000, the call holder earns a profit. If the pair closes below 1.1, the call holder earns nothing and loses the premium paid for the call.

For a put option, the trader has the right to sell the pair. If the price at settlement is trading below the strike price, the put buyer earns a profit.

OPTIONS TIPS:

- Using one of the Greek's known as Delta will give you an idea on the probability of the option expiring in the money or ITM.
- Time decay is bad for buyers, but great for sellers.
- Premiums rise when IV (implied volatility) increases. This means that buying options becomes more expensive. This can be a good time to look for selling opportunities.
- When IV is low, it may be a good time to buy options at a discount. This time usually is less than ideal to be an option seller.
- Brokers and bankers have a habit of mispricing options in their favor, which is why 90% of options expire OTM (out of the money) or

TRADING FOREX WITH OPTIONS

profitless. (Seems like a pretty high success rate if you were a seller of options.) A good strategy could be selling options when volatility is overpriced and collecting the premium

A SIMPLE STRATEGY

If I find a good opportunity to trade options, I prefer to be a seller of options. If, as noted above, 90% of options expire OTM, then this strategy seems to be highly favorable if executed properly.

The goal here is to sell short-dated OTM contracts during a time where volatility is overpriced. Time decay will be working with you, not against you, in this case. If done correctly, the contract would expire worthless, while you walk away with the overpriced premium.

WHERE TO TRADE OPTIONS

Not all brokers facilitate options trading, so you will need to look for a broker that does work with options contracts. Due to the sophistication involved in the contracts, not all brokers allow trading in options to retail traders. Brokers can provide direct access to bigger exchanges like CBOE or EUREX, or they may offer their own over the counter (OTC) contracts. The margins and fees differ for options across brokers, so be sure to look into these fees when you are looking for a broker.

Some brokers offer limited participation in options markets to retail traders, allowing them to initiate long positions and disallowing short positions due to their inherent risk. It is easy for novice traders to get carried away by a limited cost and unlimited profit potential of options. However, always be wary of the fact that not all trades are profitable, and if you get into many such trades, the payoff on one profitable trade may not be as high as the premiums paid in your many unsuccessful calls.

"The class of those who have the ability to think their own thoughts is separated by an unbridgeable gulf from the class of those who cannot"

Ludwig von Mises

TRADING FOREX
WITH FUTURES

Forex futures are currency derivative contracts whose value is based on the price of an underlying currency pair such as EUR/USD or GBP/USD. Unlike spot currency markets, the futures market is tightly regulated and standardized. Currency futures are largely similar to equity and commodity futures markets, which are traded on popular exchanges, have clearing houses to ensure trade fulfillment, and offer standardized contracts.

WHO TRADES IN THE FOREX FUTURES MARKET

The futures market is used for hedging by large and small corporations that have significant Forex exposure. The market is also used by speculators to profit from short-term and long-term movements in currency pairs.

HOW IT IS DIFFERENT FROM THE SPOT FOREX MARKET

The main difference here is that spot currencies focus on the present moment for buying and selling. Conversely, future contracts take place in the future at a different date. Unlike spot markets, currency futures markets are centralized and cannot be gamed by brokers against clients. Spot markets on the other hand are much more flexible and provide high leverage. Forex futures trade on exchanges, with the most popular being the Chicago Mercantile Exchange (CME). Forex futures require an initial margin, which depends on the size of the contract. These margins are exchange designated and, unlike in the spot markets, there is no borrowing or leverage from the broker. The initial margin acts as earnest money to ensure that parties honor the contracts.

Contracts in the futures market have expiration dates that are settled upon. Contracts expiring in the near-term are generally most active. The settlement of these trades happens after expiration with actual delivery or cash settlement of profits and losses. Day traders square off their position by entering into offsetting contracts, effectively neutralizing their exposure.

RISK MANAGEMENT IN FUTURES CONTRACTS

Exchanges have mandated specific margin requirements that traders need to maintain for their risk management. All exchanges have clearing houses that ensure all trades are settled with no transaction defaults. In addition, exchanges and clearing houses have robust mechanisms in place to withstand large turbulence.

Individual traders must manage their own portfolio risk by ensuring they do not get themselves involved in very large trades relative to their capital and follow stop losses at all times to safeguard their capital.

POPULAR CURRENCY CONTRACTS

The CME offers futures contracts on most major traded currencies, which include the following most active pairs:

EUR/USD
GBP/USD
CHF/USD
AUD/USD
CAD/USD

Apart from these pairs, contracts are available on many other currency pairs as well. All of them have varied levels of activity, though none are as high as the currency pairs listed above.

THE RUNDOWN

The dynamics of futures and spot Forex markets are not very different. Participants should take comfort in the standardization and the settlement guarantee provided by exchanges in futures trading. To ensure compliance and thoroughness, traders should check the contract specifications before initiating trades. They need to maintain enough margins, know their contract specifications beforehand, and keep their risk under control to trade profitably in futures markets.

WHY MOST TRADERS FAIL

"Risk comes from not knowing what you're doing"
-Warren Buffet

Most traders fail simply because they are gambling and not actually using a plan in their trading. They end up buying high and selling short. So, why is this? It's mainly psychological. When the price is up, traders can be eager to jump on board and try to lock in a guaranteed profit. When the price is down, they will often sell out of fear of incurring a deeper loss. Some traders may even buy more into their loss in order to bring down their average cost and attempt to capitalize on the bounce. But these behaviors can be absolutely fatal; I know this because it happened to me.

It happened when I was buying the GBP/JPY pair when it was at an extremely low level on the daily chart and experiencing a long downtrend. I was hoping for a reversal that would have led me to make a huge profit. Instead, the trend continued downward.

One thing to remember is that you don't always have to go with the trend, but you should never go against it.

I can't sit here and say that there aren't times when I am tempted to buy, hoping for a reversal. There have been times when I made lots of money averaging my cost, but there were even more times when I lost even more than I had made using the same strategy. After all, I am human and you are too (hopefully), and we are bound to make mistakes. The way to be a successful trader is to control these mistakes. Our biggest responsibility as a trader is managing risk.

When I initially started making money as an amateur trader in Forex, I didn't use stops or limits. I simply placed my bet based on a very limited bit of research and pretty much hoped the market would swing in my favor. I very often achieved profits of $500, $1,500, even over $3,000….in one day! I was starting to make some pretty decent money and, of course, I did what any brilliant investor does when they start making money with luck, I kept taking on even more risk!

The only issue was, over time, the size of my losses increased. I found myself losing $1,000, $4,000,…..$40,000…..in one day. I had no idea what was going on and was losing money much faster than I had earned it.

Essentially, my problem was that I was using way more leverage than I should have, but mostly I had my risk / reward ratio backwards. The fact that I wasn't using a stop-loss didn't help either. For example, let's say I want to take my profit at $1,000. I was setting my stop-loss (when I did use it) around $-3,000 to give myself what I thought would be enough room for the trend to get back on track and move up towards my profit region. Of course times were great when I was successful, but when this strategy failed and I lost the money, my stomach could hardly bear it. So, even though I made money in the beginning using this method, it wasn't sustainable over time. I was losing a higher amount than I had been winning.

When I was able to manage my risk better and create the opposite risk / reward ratio, I noticed an increase in my overall trading.

As a trader, your main goal is to bet in the direction that the market SHOULD go, and if it doesn't, you get out. It really is that simple. You take your quick small loss and get out. When the market DOES go in your favor, your profits should make up for all of your small losses.

Now, after years of studying and improving my trading skills, my goal is to keep losses somewhere between $-50 or $-100, while maintaining a profit of $500 to $1,000. The Law of Large Numbers will play a crucial role in the life of your trading.

"It's not whether you are right or wrong that's important, it's how much money you make when your right and how much you lose when you're wrong"
George Soros

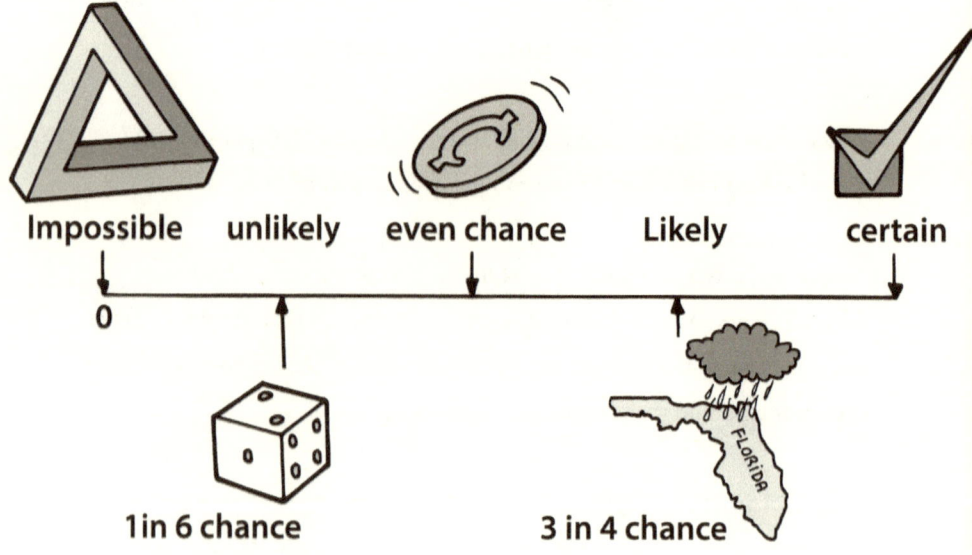

INTRO ON PROBABILITY THEORY AND THE LAW OF NUMBER SIZES

Having a good understanding of probability, I think, is one of the most important things when it comes to trading.

Probability theory is the branch of mathematics that studies probability. Probability is defined as the chance of a random event happening when there are multiple possible outcomes or set of outcomes for a given act. Probability is generally depicted by a number between 0 and 1, where 0 indicates an impossible outcome and 1 indicates a perfectly certain outcome. A simple case in point is a coin toss where one toss has two possible outcomes, heads or tails. The probability of the outcome "heads," for example, on a specific coin toss is one half (½), which means there is a 50% chance of flipping a coin and it landing on heads on one toss.

Probability is easy when the total number of samples are significant. When you run the test over a large sample size, such as 1,000 times, the odds of getting heads or tails, as in the previous coin toss example, will be close to 50:50.

However, it gets a little tricky when the outcomes are small in number. The less you flip the coin, the more difficult it will be to predict the total outcome. For example, if I flip the coin just 10 times, it could very well land on either heads or tails 7 out of the 10 times. Does this mean that either side of the coin has any type of advantage? No, the result is just due to the small sample size.

Another example I want you to keep in mind during your trading career is from the game Roulette. There are two options that are envied by many gamblers: the Black or Red, or Even or Odds bet. The goal of the strategy is to wait until there is a streak of one color, or number set, then place your bet on the opposing color or number set in the hopes that the trend reverses. If you don't get it your first time, you double up until you make your money back.

For example, say that red has come up the last 5 times. In theory, the odds of it pointing to a black digit increase over time. So, I would want to bet on black on my next turn with a small amount. If it lands on black, I win! But if it lands on red again, I simply double up the next turn and make all my money back. Unfortunately, it's not as easy as it seems, and the odds are in the dealer's favor due to the 2 additional green slots. This gives the house the upper hand with the odds of around 55:45. Going back to the law of large numbers, we know that over time we will end up the loser.

If you are looking for a book that goes more in-depth on probability theory or behavioral economics, I would highly recommend Thinking Fast and Slow by Daniel Khaneman. He is a well-respected psychologist and economist known for his work on judgement and decision making. Having a good understanding of why people make their decisions can benefit you greatly in the market.

The Black Swan Event

THE BLACK SWAN
EVENT

———————— • ▮ – █ – ▮• ————————

"Rare events are always unexpected, otherwise they would not occur"
–Nassim Taleb

There is a concept called the "Efficient Market Theory" on which most smart money managers base their investment strategies. Unfortunately, there is also something called *chaos*, which will occur from time to time. When this happens, it puts people into "panic mode," where their brains do not operate correctly. This leads to mis-pricing in the market.

Chaos brings forth times of uncertainty, which causes extremes in price action and causes tails to get fatter. This can be very disastrous for those who are not paying attention and can completely wipe out your account. Now, you may be able to make tons of money trading market swings without using a stop loss, but as we know with the law of large numbers, extremely irregular activity in the market is very possible over time.

These *rare* events will eventually come to pass; we just don't know when. The point is to exploit them when they do happen.

Warren Buffet made a very meaningful comparison to the great baseball player Ted Williams. He stated that Ted noticed his batting average increased in the areas he noted were his "sweet spot." This sweet spot was his edge. When a ball was pitched in that zone, it was more than likely to result in a hit. The only thing was though, if he chose not to swing on three pitches that were out of the sweet spot but still in the strike zone, he would be out.

When it comes to trading, you don't have strikes, but what you do have is time. This gives you the opportunity to wait for that perfect throw, pitch after pitch.

"Finance is dominated by randomness. Randomness is everything, and so because randomness is everything, you need to be uncertain."

- Ewan Kirk

TRADING PLAN

I am going to lay out the strategy that I most often follow in my trading. I always have to remember to stick exactly to the plan, otherwise it will not have good odds of success.

1. FIND OUT THE DIRECTION OF THE LARGER TREND

a. The farther you zoom out in your chart, the more reliable the chart will be. I like to zoom out to the weekly or daily time frame to get an overall idea of where the trend is going. It can also be helpful to apply the 200 day MA to help see the overall direction. The goal here is to have the wind at your back, so always remember to trade in the direction of the trend.

2. ZOOM IN AND FIND YOUR PATTERN

a. Once you have found the direction of the trend, now is the time to zoom in and find your chart pattern. This is where I use the 4 or 1 hour, or even the 30 minute chart to find a reliable pattern.

3. FIND CONFIRMATION

a. When you have found a pattern you are looking to trade, find some confirmation. Look for Support and Resistance and Moving Average Levels, as well as Bollinger Band breakouts.

4. ADJUST LEVERAGE BASED ON FUNDAMENTALS, MARKET SENTIMENT, AND TECHNICAL FACTORS

a. When trading, there are certain times to use high leverage and there are certain times to use lower leverage. The more experience you gain, the better you will get at understanding everything as a whole. A few examples are:

i. **Fundamental:** Regulation and Deregulation plays a huge part in this. Follow which opportunities or policies governments are looking to push .

ii. **Market Sentiment:** If there is the start of a new disease or some type of trade war between countries, this can affect supply chains as well as investors' risk appetite.

iii. **Technicals:** There is an old saying that prices usually revert to the mean, but we don't know exactly when. So, if price becomes largely out of whack,

most likely due to an overreaction to an event, this is a time I want to diagnose a little more. If, for example, the price of the AUD/USD pair hits a multi year low or high, this could be a time for a large reversal, or a longer continuation of the trend.

5. LET YOUR SYSTEM PLAY OUT

a. Once you have deployed your positions, let the system play out. It may take a few days or weeks, or maybe even a month or so depending on the time frame you are trading, but the goal is to ride out the wave. There may be times when you want to take a quick profit or sell for a shorter loss, but don't! This will ensure that you are consistently maximizing your profits and keeping your losses short. If you take a small profit and still take small losses, you won't get anywhere, and the system will fail.

CONCLUSION

I want to leave you with a story. There is a brief chapter from Homer's poem called *The Odyssey*. It is about Odysseus and the Island of the Sirens.

In ancient Greece, there was a legendary hero named Odysseus that lived off the coast of Athens. He was set to sail on a treacherous journey, but before doing so he met with a sorceress, named Circe, who warned him of what he would encounter on his trip. She warned him of the Sirens, which were dangerous vultures. From a distance though, they were a mere illusion of what looked like beautiful women with voices of angels.

Their singing was known to be so beautiful that it would cause the sailors to throw themselves off the ship and into the rocks, in search of the woman. This is when the sly Sirens would attack and feed on the sailors.

Circe had also told him that if you heard the singing of the Sirens and survived, that you would become wiser.

So Odysseus, being the brave warrior that he was, set off on the journey with his crew members seeking to hear the beautiful noise of the Sirens. Before they got near the Island, Odysseus had his crew tie him to the mast of the ship so he could not move. This would stop him from jumping ship. And the sailors? He had them stuff their ears with wax to prevent the sound waves from penetrating their *will-power*.

As they approached the island, the mesmerizing sound of the Sirens was tugging at Odysseus's soul. But he could not break free. He yelled and screamed to have the sailors set him free, but they would not. They stuck to the plan and the sailors survived.

Now, keep this story in mind during your trading. There are many things such as news and social media that can throw off your trading success. What has worked for us has always been keeping things simple and sticking to the plan.